# SUCCESSFULLY FAILING
## at PROCRASTINATION

# SUCCESSFULLY FAILING at PROCRASTINATION

*Understand yourself,*
*understand why you procrastinate,*
*understand how to live a better life!*

## LAUREN MIDGLEY

**COURAGE**
to Succeed

ISBN-10: 0988951800
ISBN-13: 978-0-9889518-0-8

www.LaurenMidgley.com
www.YourProcrastinationCoach.com
© 2013 Lauren Midgley

*"Nothing is as fatiguing as the eternal hanging on of an uncompleted task."*

— William James

# TABLE OF CONTENTS

# INTRODUCTION

Congratulations on taking the first step toward working on your procrastination habit. Most people joke that they are procrastinators and have been their whole life. Some people are not serious about improving their life. Since you are holding this book in your hands, it is clear you want to take action and do something about being a procrastinator!

I honor your decision and am committed to help you in any way I can.

Know that you are amongst MANY! In my *unscientific survey*, 99.95% of people on this planet (approximately 6 billion) have procrastinated at some point in their lives. The difference between you and the many others is that you are honest with yourself and know that this habit impacts your life in a negative way.

Maybe the others have resigned themselves to accept this habit and are not up for the challenge of change. Many people do not stop to think about the downsides of the procrastination habit.

What would happen if you became the go-to person to get things done, on time, and no excuses? Wouldn't it be tremendous?

As the experts in self-development say, "Change your mind, change your thoughts, and thus change your behaviors."

This book is designed to gently prod you toward shifting your thinking and behaviors. It can happen. I have seen it many times with my clients.

## WHAT ARE THE DOWNSIDES IF YOU READ THIS BOOK AND THEN TAKE NO ACTION?

If you are honest with yourself, then I am certain you could provide examples of where procrastination has negatively impacted you. Let me offer some generic examples here to stimulate your thinking:

- You paid late fees because you didn't pay your bills on time.
- You dislike organizing your home, office, or desk _____ (fill in the blank) because it takes time and is boring, and this caused you to lose your notes for an important meeting.
- You missed out on a good opportunity on _____ (fill in the blank) because you took too long to make a decision.
- You did not have a conversation with someone in a timely manner and a negative situation escalated.
- Your boss gave you a negative performance review after you consistently failed to provide needed reports or information on a timely basis.
- As a business owner, you have delayed a new product launch to your customers because it seemed so overwhelming — possibly causing you to lose sales.
- As a business owner, you delayed hiring someone to help you in your business, thinking you could do it better yourself, and then some important tasks didn't get done because you couldn't find the time.
- As a business owner, you delay confronting the unproductive employee, thinking they will improve, and the result is a decrease in profits.
- Your family is continually frustrated with you because you "promise" you will take action on _____ (fill in the blank),

but you don't get it done.

- You think you have lots of time to work on a task and then at the last minute, you are scrambling to complete it with lots of stress and bad feelings.

This book is dedicated to all who want to **FAIL SUCCESSFULLY** at procrastination and to do it really well! Stop being the PRO at **procrastination**.

I have witnessed firsthand many individuals who struggle with this habit. I know how being a procrastinator sabotages your success in many areas of your life. I am amazed at the number of people who even avoid doing things that are **good** for them.

## My Story

More than 10 years ago, I realized that this habit was significantly impacting my life. I felt on a daily basis that my life was out of control. You might recognize some of the examples I provide as behaviors and actions you do in your life. Please know I still work on "the art of focusing and **FAILING SUCCESSFULLY** at procrastination" every day.

Before I started my own coaching company in 2010, I worked as a vice president of franchise development for a franchise company in the Dallas Texas area. Each day began with the long to-do list, the schedule filled with phone calls to make, the laptop overflowing with emails to read and reply to, the calendar full of meetings to attend, and projects to complete. I truly enjoyed my work, the mission of the company, my department, the people on my team, and the tasks that needed to be done.

My biggest downfall was a lack of ability to focus on _exactly_ what needed to be accomplished. There were times when my to-do list for that day was two full pages, single spaced. I was setting myself up to fail each day by even thinking I could possibly get all those tasks done in an eight-hour day. Even with the help of a remarkable administrative assistant and productive employees in my department, I still felt quite overwhelmed on a daily basis.

The concept of having control over my day was not realistic. Like many of you, I would plan my day and be convinced I could proactively *control my day*. Then the phone would ring, the boss would stop by the office asking for information, and unexpected situations would occur all day long.

At the end of the day, I would look at my to-do list and see that maybe three to six items had been accomplished. I knew my life was in serious reactive mode … every day.

I had so much I wanted to do and accomplish. I wanted all the following (and more):
- To achieve our department monthly and annual goals
- To look good in the eyes of my peers, customers, my boss, and my boss's boss
- To move effortlessly from one meeting to another by being prepared
- To have time to make customer contacts to build relationships
- To have time to think and plan when I needed to

Those goals were just the "work side" of my life.

At home, I experienced the same feeling: that life was out of control. Deep in my heart and soul, I wanted it to be different, but it wasn't. Since I spent most of day at work (don't we all?), I had limited time at home to eat, sleep, do fun activities, read, or simply relax.

I wanted all of these things (and more):
- To have time to build a solid relationship with my spouse, kids, and extended family

- To feel that my home environment was peaceful, where I could relax
- To have time to spend on recreational activities
- To know that the finances were in order: bills paid on time, savings for the future
- To enjoy my favorite personal pastimes

The reality was that I was unfocused, running from meeting to meeting, feeling like my whole life was in chaos, not clear on the **_real_** priorities for the day. I consistently felt frustrated, highly anxious, and frazzled.

I woke up at 4 or 5 a.m. each day and felt like I was already behind. Despite that feeling, I had to press on, show up, do my best—but I knew this was an unhealthy hamster wheel. Most days, I arrived at work at 6 a.m., thinking that if I just "threw more time at this out-of-control to-do list" I could get back in control. The two hours before the others showed up for work did, in fact, provide me some uninterrupted focus time.

My workdays were filled with back-to-back meetings, 125-150 emails to respond to, and many calls to return. I knew I was drowning in detail and only able to truly respond to a certain percentage of what was coming my way.

My survival technique was to procrastinate on whichever tasks, projects, and discussions I could. If I needed more information, I could delay until I received the information. I became the queen of How to Delay. If I was not prepared for a meeting and that lack of preparation was detrimental, I would ask for the meeting to be rescheduled.

At 5 p.m. each day when the phone stopped ringing and others went home, I would breathe a sigh of relief that **_finally_** I could get back to that long to-do list. I would stay for an hour longer to wrap up the day, getting done whatever was the absolute priority for that day, and I would plan what I wanted to accomplish the next day.

Does any of this sound familiar to you?

I knew this way of life had to stop for a few reasons:

1. I knew I was not effective with the long hours, but I did not know how to break the cycle.
2. I needed to be able to say no. Yet, I was not saying no, even when it was in my best interest to do so.
3. I spent time re-creating processes, thinking that it was the process was wrong. In reality, I did not have enough time to create a checklist, template, or a routine for repetitive tasks that was well-thought out and effective.
4. I was unnecessarily frustrating others around me when I missed deadlines (in addition to myself).

I knew that it was time to take action so that I could live a more fulfilled life. I was determined to understand this habit. I found information online, read books, spoke to others who seemed to not procrastinate to find answers that would help me.

As I began to learn more about how to stop procrastinating, my "aha" moment came when I realized I easily start tasks on a project, but I am a consistent "non-finisher." As a result, I put off finishing tasks and ended up with many unfinished ones.

My excitement was in the starting of the task but NOT in the finishing. Just like many others, I would accomplish what was absolutely needed to meet a deadline, but usually at the last minute and not always in a quality fashion. If there was no formal deadline, some of those tasks remained unfinished for a long, long time.

## CAN YOU RELATE TO MY STORY AND EXAMPLES?

I continued my quest to find out why people procrastinate by studying others, interviewing them, and researching the topic extensively.

What I discovered was the reason for procrastination could be explained simply in two words: time and fear.

The concept of time relates to how people look at time and the tasks they have to accomplish.

The concept of fear is much more complex, impacted by psychological triggers you may have. You may not realize how your fears impact you from taking action.

Of the two, the element of time is much more manageable than the element of fear. Both are important. But as I have worked with clients, I have found them able to more easily adopt behaviors that impact the time aspect than behaviors that impact the fear aspect.

By changing their "time behaviors," they begin to see results, gain momentum, and are more likely to achieve success.

This book is designed to help you change behaviors and tackle the habit of procrastination. The goal is for you to enhance your awareness about your specific patterns, make decisions on what you want to change, and take action.

Think.

Plan.

Act.

Two ancillary products in this series are the audio (CDs or downloadable MP3) programs and the journal. Both help you to reinforce the results you are seeking. Additionally, free document downloads are available. You can obtain them at www.YourProcrastinationCoach.com/free-for-you. One of my favorites is the Capacity Sheet, which is my version of a to-do list that works!

The audio program provides you the highlights of this book with more real-life examples of how to overcome procrastination.

The journal encourages you to spend fifteen minutes per day to capture your thoughts, priorities, effective routines, distractions and promises made to yourself and others. When you complete fourteen days, you will have a better understanding of your habits and patterns.

If you are serious about overcoming the procrastination habit, then you will want to commit the time to learn. I recommend that you read this book two times. Yes, you read that correctly —two times. It is a quick read, filled with questions, concepts, and exercises. Do a quick read through it initially to grasp the concepts at a high level. Once you have done that, your subconscious mind will kick into gear. It will help you figure out what is important for YOU to focus on in your life and business.

Then go back and take some time to complete the exercises. Create a binder for your notes, your answers, and the free templates. If you are truly committed to changing the habit once and for all, then honor that you will need to organize your thoughts in a reference binder.

Take time between each of the chapters and the recommended exercises. Give yourself time to think about what you have learned and what you notice is going on around you in your life. There is no need to rush through this process.

Changing your thinking and your behaviors will take time. Some small changes will come quickly, but long-term results will take some time and reprogramming of how you have always done things.

The questions are meant to be thought provoking.

To maximize your learning, allow time to absorb the information as you do each exercise. Make a commitment to do some quality thinking, to read what you have written, to take action, and to begin seeing results.

Throughout this book, I refer to templates for you to use. Feel free to download them (they are complimentary) from my website at www.YourProcrastinationCoach.com/free-for-you. By doing so, you can print off extra worksheets to use over and over again as procrastination reoccurs in your life (and it will, trust me!).

Take time to create your *Successfully Failing at Procrastination* three-ring binder, to hold the templates and your notes. Doing so will maximize your learning and support your success. Use a binder that has a pocket inside, so that you can keep this book there.

If you want to dig deeper to receive more personalized help, then check out chapter 7 on Next Steps to Take.

I have found that meeting with like-minded individuals who share similar goals and challenges can be very effective in catapulting your learning and changing behaviors. For a schedule of virtual workshops, go to www.YourProcrastinationCoach.com.

If you have any difficulty with downloading the material, please email me at Lauren@LaurenMidgley.com.

My goal is for you to **SUCCESSFULLY FAIL** at procrastination so you can lead a better life, without those hurtful feelings of guilt, frustration, and being overwhelmed. I want you to see significant results.

Additionally, I hope you will return to this book when you get stuck as new procrastination challenges arise in your life. Know that I am in your corner and willing to help you. Consider sharing this information with others who struggle with this habit. Encourage them to tackle this habit.

Each time you read through the material, you will

understand the procrastination habit on new levels and achieve greater success. Repetition of helpful behavior is positive reinforcement!

Face the fact that procrastination was learned. You were not born a procrastinator. You do not have to be a procrastinator for the rest of your life. What habits you now have are learned; you can unlearn them with focus, time, and attention.

Begin getting what you want without the effects of procrastination. Develop your skills for producing consistently without delay or guilt! You can do this.

Lauren Midgley
Your Procrastination Coach

Chapter

1

"*While we are postponing, life speeds by.*"
— Seneca, *Roman Statesman*

## GETTING STARTED

**When I began** studying the habit of procrastination, I realized it has the ability to impact lives in a BIG way. Many negative adjectives are associated with procrastination:

Feeling overwhelmed, guilty, frustrated, embarrassed, depressed, debilitated, weakened, drained of energy, anxious, fearful—and the list goes on and on. It seemed that if you were procrastinating in one area of your life that was also happening in many other areas of life: work, relationships, physical environment, body, health, finances, unfulfilled dreams, to name a few.

Only you can determine which area has the highest priority at this point in your life. The reality is you cannot effectively work on all of them at once.

The purpose of this book is to teach you a process—or way of thinking—so that no matter what area of your life seems to be overwhelming or out of control, you will have a way to work through it.

As you will see, overcoming procrastination starts with

becoming aware, challenging your beliefs, changing routines and habits, reflecting on whether those changes worked for you, and then adding a solid dose of commitment!

## MAKING THE COMMITMENT TO OVERCOME PROCRASTINATION

A quote by Bill Blackman, the president of the Hearts and Minds Network, says:

> *"Great changes may not happen right away, but with effort even the difficult may become easy."*

How many times do we know our plate is full, but we keep adding to it? Did we forget how to say NO?

We either delay or we don't make the commitment or we say YES to too many things. The real issue here is that we forget to consider how important it is to balance what we say YES to and what we say NO to in our lives.

*How many times do we know our plate is full but we keep adding to it?*

There are many reasons making a commitment can be scary. The most basic one is that if we make a commitment, then we have "stuck our neck out" and know we need to *honor* that commitment. The "honor" part of that statement is particularly compelling.

If we have told others about our commitment, then we feel good when we fulfill that commitment or we feel bad if we fail to fulfill it.

Of course, many times a public commitment is not honored.

## THE SIZE OF OUR PLATE

So let's think about what leads up to making the commitment and taking it off the "plate of procrastination." When the plate is truly full, how do we know that?

If we are truly honest with ourselves and look at the "plate," we know the plate holds a variety of unfinished tasks, incomplete projects, or unmet goals.

For some of us, that plate may be the size of a Christmas dinner platter, and for others it might be the size of a child's tea set saucer.

Whatever the size of the plate, those procrastinated items reside happily on the plate in our heads until an action is taken.

Does a visual of the size of the plate in our head help us?

Many of my clients are visual learners. Initially, I ask this question: How big is your plate now? Do you want to increase its size, make it smaller, or have it stay the same? Most answer that they want a smaller, more manageable plate.

## EXERCISE #1 – *What are You Procrastinating On, Right Now?*

First, create a list of your procrastinated items. Keep in mind this is NOT tomorrow's to-do list. It actually is the list of those tasks, projects, discussions, goals, dreams that live in your head rent-free. List the bigger items you know you have delayed for some time.

A good clue about what items to list: When you think about them, you feel those "yukky" feelings: **F**rustrated, **O**verwhelmed, and **G**uilty. I refer to these as FOG. FOG creates a state of confusion and bewilderment. In this state, no wonder we don't take action. A definition of fog is: obscuring haze that limits vision. Yes, our vision is limited.

My client, Mary, found it freeing to create a list of ALL the procrastination items she had in her head. The physical act of writing them on paper freed up space in her head. With a piece of lined paper, she did a brain dump in a space of 15 minutes. She went back to the list a few days later to add more.

What specific items are you procrastinating on RIGHT NOW?

1. _____

2. _____

3. _____

4. _____

5. _____

6. _____

## CLEARING OUT SPACE

A momentary sense of relief came to Mary when she knew she had captured most of the items all in one place. Some items were small; some were big.

An example of her list:

1. Organize the garage (extremely cluttered with many items that could be sold on eBay or craigslist)

2. File a claim with a third-party claim company—worth $500 to her, gaining some needed dollars

3. Have a long, overdue conversation with a friend—the last conversation ended in a fight, feeling bad every time she thinks of this situation

4. Write an article for a trade journal in which she is featured as a monthly columnist—knowing that it will jeopardize her relationship with the editor

5. Finalize her marketing brochure—getting the copyedits and head-shot photo done, resulting in new clients and revenue

6. Talk to and hire a virtual assistant to help her in her business —freeing her up for more productive activities

As you can see, the entries relate to her business and her

personal life.

However, once she had the list created, she soon felt overwhelmed by it all. Her first thoughts were, "How will I get this all done? I simply do not have the time."

In reality, she did find the time but it took focus, intention, and a shift in thinking.

Consider this analogy: If you were to look at all the activities you do in a month's time and list them on a giant page posted on a large wall, you would be overwhelmed. Thank goodness we don't need to do that. That month-at-a-glance view IS overwhelming. Trust me, your head would hurt!

Instead of thinking big on this, I asked Mary to capture the "top of mind" procrastination items on one page. The purpose was twofold:

1. To free up some space in her head
2. To understand which ones were bothering her

The way to think about all those tasks, projects, and goals she had in her head: They were occupying valuable "real estate in her brain" and contributing to FOG—feeling Frustrated, Overwhelmed, and Guilty. When too many items are on the "procrastination plate," it weighs us down and impacts our ability to think clearly and take action.

In our coaching session, it was clear to me that her ability to be creative (and she is one of the most creative people I know) was stunted by these procrastinated items. By creating the list, Mary permitted her mind to rest. She found it to be a huge relief.

Once you create your list of six

*When too many items are on the "procrastination plate," it weighs us down and impacts our ability to think clearly and take action.*

to eight items, answer another question:

Which one item is **screaming** the loudest to be worked on **first**? Write it down.

* * * * *

For Mary, once she looked at the list, that item jumped out at her. She clearly understood she did not need to work on the other five items immediately. Instead, she began to intentionally focus and think about the next steps on that ONE item.

And she committed.

And she took action.

**Yes, the old axiom of breaking it down into manageable pieces <u>does</u> work.**

The way she took action is important. Mary **accepted** two major concepts in this exercise.

1. To work on just one of the six items
2. To take only TWO action steps on that priority item and to commit ONLY ONE hour of time in the next day or two to begin the process

Based on those two factors, she was ready to take on those two action items, thinking, "Okay, this is doable."

You, too, will want to get to the same mindset of, "Okay, I can do this."

For those of you who are curious, the one Mary selected was submitting the claim to gain a much-needed $500.

When I asked why she had procrastinated on that item when clearly it benefited her wallet, her response was that there were six different places she needed to locate information in order to submit the claim. She thought it would take her HOURS to complete this task. In reality, it only took her 90 minutes.

Are you ready to make your "Procrastination-at-a-Glance" list?

Are you ready to tackle that ONE item screaming at you to get it done?

Okay, then it is time to commit.

And take action.

Go do it.

## SOMEDAY IS NOT A DAY OF THE WEEK

Recently I saw the quote below while online and thought it was perfect for those who claim that *someday, they will do* _____ (fill in the blank).

The quote says,

> *"They said that procrastination was the source of all my sorrow. I don't know what that big word means. I will look it up tomorrow."* Author unknown

We have all used the phrase "someday I will do _____." Ask yourself, "When will that someday ever happen?" For some people, it will happen because they make it happen. For others, the "someday" does not happen due to their procrastination or lack of commitment.

Whenever I drive by a cemetery, I am reminded that some people who reside there did not see their dreams come to fruition. How sad.

Whose fault is it when our dreams do not happen? It is our own fault. When we are in charge of each day and of our choices, then it is no one else's fault.

We have the option to take action.

The definition of procrastination in the Merriam-Webster dictionary is:

> "to put off intentionally the doing of something that should be done."

Sounds simple, doesn't it?

## WHAT PROCRASTINATION IS NOT

Procrastination is NOT just a time-management issue. If it were that easy, we all would simply write down what we have to do in our planners and do it.

Procrastination is NOT you being lazy. In fact, many procrastinators lead a busy life.

Procrastination is NOT an insignificant habit—as it costs you in ways you probably haven't thought of.

Procrastination is NOT simple. "Just do it" is easier said than done. The phrase alone rarely will motivate someone to NOT procrastinate. No, there is usually more to the story about why we intentionally put off doing something.

To work on procrastination, you have to be willing to think about your beliefs, your actions, your habits— and most important, be willing to change.

Are you ready? If not now, then when will you be?

## THE CONSEQUENCES OF PROCRASTINATING ON OUR DREAMS

*"The young have aspirations that never come to pass; the old have reminiscences of what never happened."*

— Hector Hugh Munro, *British novelist*

Every day we have decisions to make and problems to solve. That is just how life rolls. Think about all the decisions you make every day, from small ones to large ones.

Some of the decisions have our undivided attention.

Some of the decisions do not. So how do we discern which ones deserve our time and attention?

Two words: PAIN and CONSEQUENCES.

We assess the situation and determine:

If I take this action, then it is resolved and I am done with it.

I know what to do and take action.

Or

I choose to delay this action because I need more information, or the steps to completion are not clear, or I am avoiding conflict. A confused mind generally chooses to take NO ACTION. But the issue still resides in my head as an unfinished to-do item.

## THREE REASONS WE DON'T TAKE ACTION

If we think about our dreams, our aspirations, those someday goals, then why do we procrastinate taking action? Generally, these topics are positive and different than the day-to-day decisions we face.

1. The concept of pain or consequences is not usually thought of or associated with the concept of our DREAMS. One thinks there are no consequences if a dream is not fulfilled. Or said another way, "I can't fail if I don't act on my dream, so I will just talk about it as a someday goal."
2. The dreams can be large projects or goals … and have not been broken down into actionable, smaller tasks.
3. Maybe it *is* just a dream … and you are not serious or committed about taking action. Ever.

For example, I had a client who wanted to start his own business. He had that dream for at least 20 years but always had fear about moving forward. When I asked what held him back, he had many concerns such as finances, lack of support from his wife, marketplace competition, to name a few. He offered many excuses. So how committed was he to his dream? If all he did was talk about it and he took no action, when was it going to happen? If not now, then when?

## Moving Forward

So, what needs to happen to move a dream forward?
Have you made a decision to move ahead with starting your own business or _____ (fill in the blank), or is it just living in your head as an idea?

Thoughts generate ideas which generate action which generates fulfillment of dreams. What will motivate you to move that dream from an idea state to an actual plan with action steps?

## Suggestions to End the Procrastination on Your Dream

1. Schedule personal time with yourself to focus on that specific question. Brainstorm all the tasks needed to make that one dream happen. Capture your thoughts on paper. The process of writing will help to organize your thoughts. It is only a draft at this point. Perfection is not needed.

2. Create a visual to capture the images, colors, and words of your dream.

3. Talk with someone you trust about your dream. Ask them to help you brainstorm and hold you accountable for at least five small steps to get started in a specific time frame.

4. Create a binder to capture all your thoughts about this dream or aspiration. Refer to it frequently. Daily is a good idea!

5. If possible, find a way to live the dream as a temporary state ...acting as if...so you can experience it with no strings attached.

Think about how it makes you feel to have unfulfilled dreams. Does it make you anxious?

Delaying on day-to-day problems, issues, or decisions is a conscious choice.

So is procrastinating on your dream.

What if you associated a pseudo pain or consequence with your unmet dream to convince yourself to take action?

Would that motivate you to begin action on it?

Three questions to ask yourself:

1. When can I schedule time to capture my dream on paper?
2. Whom can I share that information with to help me get started?
3. What is the personal cost if I do not follow through on my dream?

Your aspirations are important to your inner self. Finding a way to take action is worth the thought time. You CAN do this. Jot down some notes on what are your next action steps toward fulfilling your dreams.

*"The individual who wants to reach the top in business must appreciate the might and force of habit. He must be quick to break those habits that can break him— and hasten to adopt those practices that will become the habits that help him achieve the success he desires."*

— Jean Paul Getty, *American businessman*

## THINK ABOUT WHAT YOU DON'T PROCRASTINATE ON

**The journey of** dealing with procrastination can start with looking on the positive side. There ARE areas in your life where you DON'T procrastinate. We are not always aware of those areas where procrastinating would be the last thing we would do.

Instead we label ourselves as a procrastinator and think that applies to all areas of our life. I believe that is not the case.

Begin thinking of tasks you do in your life now, those tasks it would NEVER cross your mind to procrastinate.

Example: You are paid on the 1st and 15th of the month. You pay bills on the 1st and 15th. You always do this, have done it for years, and would NEVER think of changing this routine. Paying a late fee on a bill seems crazy to you.

Example: You are always on time for work. You would never think of being late. In fact, generally you prefer to be there just a bit early and feel uncomfortable if you are late.

Example: You enjoy going for a walk every evening in your neighborhood for at least 30 minutes. You like how you feel afterwards. The good feeling occurs on several levels—physically, mentally, and emotionally. If you don't do your walk, then you feel as though you have missed it.

Example: When given an assignment at work, you are conscious of the deadline. You create a mini-calendar showing milestones for when certain phases need to be completed. If you are behind on the project midway through, you will work a few extra hours to catch up. Or you will creatively think of resources to help you with this assignment. Or you will communicate to those who need to know of the delay.

Example: After a networking event, you always allow time for follow-up, through phone calls, emails, or other marketing methods. In fact, this is so important to you that you make time in your calendar to do this…for each networking event you attend. When you arrive back at your office, either you or your assistant will enter the names of the people you met into your contact database. You like having their information at your fingertips.

Example: Around the house, you have a checklist of tasks handling a specific chore, usually associated with your calendar. The chore could be tracking the regular watering of the plants, or capturing the date you replace the air filters, or maintaining the schedule of when the exterminator comes quarterly. To run your household efficiently, you have mastered this checklist and calendaring process.

Example: You fear running out of gas, because it happened to you once. When it happened, it was inconvenient and a bit scary to correct the situation. Now you NEVER let the gas tank be lower than one-quarter full.

Example: You had a computer crash on your business laptop. Luckily, you had backed up the information the week before, so you lost a minimal amount of data. Now, you make sure you have your data backed up on a daily or weekly basis, without fail!

Do some of these examples seem to be "right on" or ridiculous? In reality, these examples represent systems you have in place to effectively help you manage these tasks.

How one feels about their tasks relates to their beliefs and the importance of those tasks.

Take fifteen to thirty minutes to think about areas in your life where you would NOT procrastinate*. Your entries might be from these areas: personal, work, relationships, finances, health, or school. Try to think of at least five examples.

## EXERCISE #2 – *Areas that I Never Procrastinate and Why*

Take time to complete each page on what you do NOT procrastinate on, as it relates to:

- Tasks
- Goals
- Projects
- Discussions
- Decisions

*These worksheets is available at www.YourProcrastination-Coach.com/free-for-you.

Review what you have written.

Now spend another fifteen minutes to capture your insights about the statements you wrote. Dig deep to understand WHY you do not procrastinate on these tasks. It is important for you to realize there are areas of your life where you do NOT procrastinate.

## TASKS

| Those tasks that I tackle immediately – without delay: | The reason I NEVER procrastinate on this task is: |
|---|---|
| 1. | |
| 2. | |
| 3. | |
| 4. | |
| 5. | |
| 6. | |
| 7. | |
| 8. | |
| 9. | |
| 10. | |

## GOALS

| Those goals that I work on consistently | The reason I NEVER procrastinate on this goal is: |
|---|---|
| 1. | |
| 2. | |
| 3. | |
| 4. | |
| 5. | |
| 6. | |
| 7. | |
| 8. | |
| 9. | |
| 10. | |

## PROJECTS

| Those projects that I work on —without delay | The reason I NEVER procrastinate on this project is: |
|---|---|
| 1. | |
| 2. | |
| 3. | |
| 4. | |
| 5. | |
| 6. | |
| 7. | |
| 8. | |
| 9. | |
| 10. | |

## DISCUSSIONS

| Those discussions that I have—without delay | Who are the discussions with, generally? |
|---|---|
| 1. | |
| 2. | |
| 3. | |
| 4. | |
| 5. | |
| 6. | |
| 7. | |
| 8. | |
| 9. | |
| 10. | |

## DECISIONS

| Those decisions that I make quickly: | The reason I don't procrastinate on this type of decision is: |
|---|---|
| 1. | |
| 2. | |
| 3. | |
| 4. | |
| 5. | |
| 6. | |
| 7. | |
| 8. | |
| 9. | |
| 10. | |

Acknowledge and celebrate that success!

The secrets of your success for NOT procrastinating in these areas generally relate to two main ideas:

1. You have adopted this belief system, accepted it wholeheartedly, and believe it to be important in your life to be consistent.

2. You created a system or routine, and you allow it to operate on autopilot when it comes to this specific task, goal, project, decision, or discussion. Your habit is well formed.

***Key learning: Your current good habits, established systems, and core beliefs impact your actions. Continually reinforce good habits to continue them.***

Key Questions:

1. How do your established habits and core beliefs impact your actions?

_____

_____

_____

_____

2. How might you apply the insights you listed above to a key task you ARE procrastinating on right now in your life or business?

_____

_____

_____

_____

## Do You Have Clarity?

*"If you are talented but unfocused, it's difficult to succeed because you're moving in a thousand directions. Your path is not purposeful ... it's chaotic."*
— John C. Maxwell, *American clergyman*

Without clarity on the specific topic you are procrastinating on, you will be reluctant to take action.

"Clarity" seems like an overworked term in today's world. Yet is it important. Why? You will likely procrastinate if you do not have a clear picture of what action you want to take or the direction you want your business to go.

So let's define clarity for our purposes here: your vision of what you want, why you want to do it, and how you intend to begin the first steps.

If the "what, why, and how" are not answered or are not clear, then you will not be motivated to move forward.

So how do you get **your** clarity?

The "why" is important to pay attention to—as it shapes your belief system.

Suppose you don't have that clarity. How do you get to that "why"?

There are a variety of ways:

- Invest in some dedicated thinking time.
- Brainstorm with your team or an accountability partner.
- Define the problem and list all possible solutions.
- Converse with trusted advisors who have expertise.
- Put pen to paper to list what you ARE clear on, then determine what you still need answers on.

## EXERCISE #3 - *Visioning the Options*

Which of five bullet points listed will work for you?

_____

_____

Go back to your number one procrastination item listed on page sixteen.

Take time to answer these questions.

What is my vision of what I want?

_____

_____

Why do I want to do this task?

_____

List a few first steps to get started:

1. _____

2. _____

3. _____

## WHEN IS ENOUGH...ENOUGH?

How clear is clear **enough**? Depending on the topic you are wrestling with, you may not have all the answers, but you may have most of them. Let's say that you have 80% of the answers.

If your desired goal is to take action, then set a deadline.

Be clear with yourself that you will tackle this and will take action steps.

As business coach Mike Litman says, "You don't have to get it right; you just have to get it going."

## THE REALITY OF BECOMING READY TO TAKE THE LEAP

*"Things can fall apart, or threaten to, for many reasons, and then there's got to be a leap of faith. Ultimately, when you're at the edge, you have to go forward or backward; if you go forward, you have to jump together."*

— Yo-Yo Ma

Have you ever been in a vicious cycle in your head? You feel like you have to take action on a specific task, but nothing is happening. Yet you feel stirred up. You hesitate to bring your fear to the surface. So what happens?

The vicious cycle of constant thought that goes round and round in your head with no end in sight.

## WATCHING OTHERS TAKE ACTION

My client, Joan, has a great deal of fear about making a job change. She knows she should take action since her company was recently sold. She knows she could lose her position, has seen other valuable employees quit, and yet remains frozen in place. As her coworkers leave the company one by one, she musters the courage to begin to explore many options out there. Should she start her own consultancy company? Should she go to work for the competitor? Should she stay with her current company, even though her position might be at risk?

The more she thinks about her options, the more energized she becomes. She gathers lots of details, talks to many people to hear their thoughts, and then she becomes distracted. She is stuck, frozen in place once again. The familiar feeling of being overwhelmed is back.

Making a change is unthinkable…still.

## How Do You Realistically Break the Cycle?

When you are ready to make a change, you will. The hesitation and resistance is telling you that you are NOT ready. Trying to break a cycle when you are not ready could end up with disastrous results.

Instead, notice the resistance. Accept the hesitation. Go around the circle a few more times. Eventually, you will break free all on your own. When you do, you will be so ready. Just acknowledge to yourself that you would NOT have been ready any sooner.

Chapter

**3**

*"How different our lives are when we really know what is deeply important to us, and keeping that picture in mind, we manage ourselves each day to be and to do what really matters most."*

— Steven R. Covey, *American author*

## VISUALIZE A LIFE WITHOUT PROCRASTINATION

**Everyone procrastinates to** some degree. Very few people are free from this habit. How do you define procrastination, as it relates to you?

A simple definition of procrastination is:

"putting off or delaying something that needs immediate attention."

I would make the case that "immediate" may not always be a factor. Sometimes we delay on something important but not always urgent. We tell ourselves we know we shouldn't delay but we delay anyway. From keeping New Year's resolutions to getting a new job to paying bills on time, we can always find a reason or excuse to put something off.

Oftentimes, the reason we procrastinate is a lack of desire to do the task. We just don't like the task or have the interest to do it.

But are you aware of the real toll procrastination is taking on your life? Most procrastinators don't realize the REAL costs associated with their actions.

As we looked at in chapter 2, you can procrastinate on a task, goal, project, decision, or discussion.

It's possible you may not be procrastinating at all, but rather you are affected by the following:

1. Too many tasks on your to-do list
2. Inability to focus and concentrate to get things done
3. Lack of clarity due to not enough information to move forward

The assumption is that the procrastinator is not affected by these types of things but is willfully not doing what they know they should do.

Having too many tasks, goals or projects on your list is not a classic definition of procrastination but rather can result from an inability to say no. It could also result from your lack of ability to understand your time available versus tasks you undertake to do.

Inability to focus and concentrate may signal a need to minimize distractions. Understand what distracts you and then create the environment to keep distractions to a minimum.

Lack of clarity on a tasks, goals or projects simply means you cannot move forward without obtaining information you need for clarity. The best path here is to focus on getting the necessary information and then move forward.

## EXERCISE #4 – *More Visioning of Life Without Procrastination*

Take at least fifteen to thirty minutes to answer the following questions.

These questions are in template form at my website: www.YourProcrastinationCoach.com/free-for-you

Make sure you are in a location where there will be no interruptions. For this exercise, you want to be able to visualize, imagine, explore, be nonjudgmental, and have a clear, open mind. Turn on relaxing music. Drink your favorite beverage. Put your feet up. Be relaxed and set up the right environment for creativity.

What would your life look like if you did not procrastinate? Write out all the benefits you would derive, such as personal satisfaction, improved relationships, less anxiety, feeling more in control. Write as much as you can.

_____

_____

_____

_____

_____

_____

If you had NO procrastination in your life, how would you feel? Describe in detail. For example, it might feel like the opposite of the following adjectives: stressed, not at ease, uptight, feel bad around friends/family, unhappy, out of control, not accomplished.

What words would you use?

_____

_____

_____

_____

_____

_____

What feedback would you get from others close to you if you did not procrastinate or did a better job of not procrastinating? What would be their exact words to you?

_____

_____

_____

_____

_____

Who is the one person who would notice the most if you were not procrastinating?

_____

_____

_____

_____

_____

Write your personal vision statement that defines what not procrastinating in your key area would feel like. Use some of your thoughts from the previous questions.

_____

_____

_____

_____

_____

_____

In what areas of your life do you procrastinate the most? (Some ideas: job, developing relationships, physical environment, maintaining relationships, health, body, finances, pursuing your passions/dreams, and many more.)

_____

_____

_____

_____

_____

_____

What is something you are procrastinating on at this moment? Describe it in detail.

_____

_____

_____

_____

_____

_____

List some of the consequences you have experienced or might experience as a result of this procrastination.

_____

_____

_____

_____

_____

_____

*Key learning:*

*The more clearly you can describe the picture of what your life will look like without procrastination as an impacting habit, the greater your chance of success at managing it. Reread the vision statement you wrote. Now read it out loud. If it still feels fuzzy, then keep thinking, refining, and rewriting your words until you are satisfied you have captured your vision.*

*If you are brave, read it to the person whose name you listed above for their reaction.*

*Type it out. Post it someplace you'll see it, like on your bathroom mirror, your computer, or your desk.*

*The visual reminder will help you change behavior.*

Key Questions:

1. Has your awareness of your day-to-day procrastination habits been heightened? If yes, how so?

_____

_____

_____

_____

_____

_____

2. Are you beginning to understand the impact procrastination in general has on your life? Describe the impact.

_____

_____

_____

_____

_____

_____

## WHAT IS REALLY HOLDING YOU BACK?

*"Nothing in the world can take the place of persistence. Talent will not; nothing is more common than unsuccessful men with talent. Genius will not; unrewarded genius is almost a proverb. Education will not; the world is full of educated derelicts. Persistence and determination alone are omnipotent. The slogan 'Press On' has solved and always will solve the problems of the human race."*

— Calvin Coolidge, *American President*

Persistence means you keep moving toward your goal even when you feel like quitting.

A key element of moving forward is keeping your vision of what you want to accomplish clear in your mind. Sometimes you need to have that vision in a place where it is visible…so you see it.

Perhaps it would help to have a Goal Sheet posted where you will see it and absorb it every day.

Think of your life as being on a trajectory like a rocket. There are three ways this rocket of life will travel.

## Which Path is Yours?

PATH ONE: Crisis. There is continual crisis with lots of drama. Everything seems to go wrong. You feel like you just cannot get on the right track. You struggle. Life is difficult and it doesn't let up. The crises keep coming your way.

PATH TWO: Chance. Occasionally, you find that chance works in your favor, that good things happen to you. Some projects get done, some promotions happen, some additional dollars fall into your pocket. Life isn't quite so hard, but it still feels like it is hit or miss. Some good luck happens but not nearly enough.

PATH THREE: Choice. You are conscious of your choices. You know what you want. You know where you want your life to take you. Your "systems" are in place. You know struggles will come your way, but you are ready to take them on as they occur. You choose self-development as a way of life. You choose to be productive and not let tasks, goals, or projects linger. In general, you feel good about your direction and the speed of your trajectory.

You may not want a balance of these paths!

The reality for many of us is that we live with a bit of each of these three paths in our lives.

The question is: Are these sections equal, or some smaller, or some larger?

You probably have not thought about your life with these three labels attached.

Take a moment to assign a percent value to each of the three, such as 10% Crisis, 30% Chance, and 60% Choice.

## EXERCISE #5 – *Your Balance Path Percentages*

What ARE your percentages today?

_____ Crisis _____Chance _____ Choice

What do you want your percentages to be in the future?

_____ Crisis _____Chance _____ Choice

Describe what would need to happen to begin the shift of those percentages.

_____

_____

_____

_____

_____

Using the concept from the above quote by Calvin Coolidge: How will you "press on" from what is holding you back?

_____

_____

_____

_____

_____

## IMPACT OF BRICK WALLS ON YOUR MOTIVATION

*"You have to find something that you love enough to be able to take risks, jump over the hurdles, and break through the brick walls that are always going to be placed in front*

*of you. If you don't have that kind of feeling for what*
*it is you are doing, you'll stop at the first giant hurdle."*
— Author unknown

Have you ever started out on a project, all gung ho, ready to take it all on? Have you ever been so excited that you could see yourself finishing early and having done an outstanding job?

And so you started down the path to create the project plan and timelines, identify the major milestones, and gather the key resources (money and people). You thought of nothing else except this project. It was part of your core to see this project through to completion and success.

## TRIPPED UP BY THE BRICK WALL

And then all of a sudden, you run smack into the brick wall that brings the project momentum to a screeching halt. You stop, shake your head, and pick yourself up from the dirt, asking what the heck just happened. You thought you had anticipated all the pitfalls of what could go wrong.

You tell yourself it is okay and you just need time to solve this newly cropped-up problem. It is time to figure out how to get around this obstacle.

## WHEN CONFIDENCE FALTERS

Self doubt easily creeps in, when confidence falters. This scenario is common. You begin to question your plan, your strategy, and your desired outcome. Critics come out of the woodwork like cockroaches to tell you all the things you are doing wrong. You stop taking action. Your momentum is gone.

When this begins to occur, you need to have some strong self-talk to snap you out of this funk. Otherwise, you will be off track quickly, with procrastination and lack of motivation sure to occur.

Don't let that happen. You are better than that! Regain that "love" of the project to see you through to the end!

How do you do that?

You re-read your original plan, timelines and mission. You realize you cannot go "through" some obstacles. Instead, you find ways to "go around", to re-capture the momentum. Otherwise, procrastination will impact your efforts.

Chapter

4

*"When you do nothing, you feel overwhelmed and powerless. But when you get involved, you feel the sense of hope and accomplishment that comes from knowing you are working to make things better."*

— Author unknown

## SEE YOUR WHOLE PICTURE AT A GLANCE

**The areas you** habitually procrastinate on are totally unique to you. Each person procrastinates in their own way.

Most of the details of these (if not all) areas reside in your head…probably causing you angst. Remember those emotions you feel about your unfinished items discussed earlier. It is likely you have not written ALL the unfinished items down. By writing all those items on paper, you will be on the path to feeling much better.

Getting this information out of your head and onto paper has several benefits:

1. Immediately reduces the mental clutter
2. Relieves some emotional anxiety
3. Allows you to look at all the areas at once, thus helping you prioritize

By seeing your whole picture and its impact on your life, you can begin to address what you want to work on first, second, third, and so on. Once you see the list in its entirety, you can make some decisions.

What type of decisions?

You may have been procrastinating on a task, goal, project, discussion, or dream, but in reality, it does not need to be done or could be done by someone else. Or it may be that you can intentionally procrastinate on it, knowing you have a few areas that need more immediate attention.

Intentional procrastination is determining "yes, I need to do that task…but I am intentionally delaying it until either X happens or Y date." By doing so, you are acknowledging it still needs to be accomplished, but not immediately. Capturing it in writing helps you to not forget and to not avoid doing it at some point in the future.

## EXERCISE #6 – *Benefits of the Procrastination Log*

In this exercise, you will need 30–60 minutes to fully complete this matrix, known as the Procrastination Log. Use the space provided here to enter your answers or feel free to download the template from www.YourProcrastinationCoach.com/free-for-you.

Once you have finished it, set it aside. Go back to it a few days later. Review and revise. Again, your subconscious mind will continue to work on it, thinking about these areas. More thoughts will come to you as you look at it a second time.

The key benefit of this one-page Log is that your key areas of procrastination are all listed in one place.

Seeing them all on one page allows your mind to absorb the bigger picture. The more time you spend looking at it, the more it will become clear which area is the priority.

Use the Log as an ongoing reference page, updating it periodically.

## Procrastination Log

| What are you procrastinating on now! List them out in random order – Decision, task, project or goal | Need to Start(s) or Need to Finish(f) | Rate the level of importance in your overall life/business Use 1-10 scale with 10 being the highest | What tasks do you do work on instead of the desired one? | What feelings come up for you when you think about the uncompleted | What are the consequences if you do not do this? | What are the benefits on completing this item? |
|---|---|---|---|---|---|---|
| 1 | | | | | | |
| 2 | | | | | | |
| 3 | | | | | | |
| 4 | | | | | | |
| 5 | | | | | | |
| 6 | | | | | | |
| 7 | | | | | | |
| 8 | | | | | | |

# KEYS TO COMPLETING THE PROCRASTINATION LOG:

1. Complete column 1 first (moving down the page). List one item in each square. It is okay to use just one or two words to describe each item. Take the approach that you want to clear your brain of ALL the procrastinated items first; this is a "brain dump" of all those tasks, activities, goals, projects, decisions, and discussions.

2. Remember this is NOT a to-do list but rather those bigger tasks that consistently are not being done and need some type of resolution. It is fine to list items in random order; you will rank them later.

3. Look at each item in column 1 and begin to fill in the boxes from left to right, answering the questions for each square in that row:

   a. Do you need to start or finish this item?

   b. What level of importance does this item hold in your overall life or business? Assign it a priority number.

   c. List the distracting tasks you work on instead of the desired one.

   d. Record the feelings that arise when you think about the procrastinated item. Do you have anxiety, fear, frustration, confusion, or rejection?

   e. List the consequences of not completing the procrastinated item.

   f. List the benefits of completing this item.

To fill this Procrastination Log completely may take some time. You may want to take a few sessions to finalize this.

## FEELING OVERWHELMED

*"When you do nothing, you feel overwhelmed and power-less. But when you get involved, you feel the sense of hope and accomplishment that comes from knowing you are working to make things better."*

—Author unknown

Yes. They hang out together. I've seen them (the evil twins called Overwhelm and Powerless) being best friends for a long time—and so have you.

Are you feeling overwhelmed frequently…to the point that you are absolutely worn down physically and mentally?

Feeling that way is a choice. Your choice.

It impacts not only you but also others around you. Family and friends know when you are overwhelmed. Because of their love for you, it bothers them too, as they do not want to see you in that difficult state. They want to help you, but often do not know how.

Yes, stop right now with the thoughts of being overwhelmed and accepting that your life has to be this way. It doesn't.

Who has the choice to deal with the "overwhelm"? You.

Easier said (or written, in this case!) than done. But think about it…who else in your life will take away the "overwhelm"? Consider how unloving this state of being is for you. You know you deserve better than that. But…you must decide and choose to shift your thoughts and truly think differently.

## TIME TO LET GO

Begin by "letting go" or "giving permission to" your mind to consider your overwhelming situation differently.

Consider this reality from the opposite direction. Doing so requires a conscious effort on your part to consider that you can manage this overwhelming situation and you can control it.

By changing your feeling and emotion surrounding this situation, you can start with your belief that it can be different.

## EXERCISE #7 – *What Seems Overwhelming Right Now?*

Take fifteen minutes to write down the three to five things overwhelming you most right now. Capturing them on paper gets them out of your head and helps you to look at them objectively.

1. _____

2. _____

3. _____

4. _____

5. _____

To the right of each item on your list, add two other pieces of information:

1. How do I feel about this task? _____

2. How long will it take to complete this task? _____

Capture those emotions. After you have written your thoughts down, then STOP again. Reread these items from a loving point of view, rather than one of desperation or beating yourself up over not having accomplished them.

It does work.

Oftentimes, our sense of being overwhelmed stems from the emotions swirling around in our heads, perceived lack of time, and possible lack of desire to do any of the delayed tasks or projects. The act of stopping, letting go, and writing out the thoughts and emotions in your head helps manage the mind chatter. My prediction is that you will have a clearer head and feel much better.

Overwhelm and Powerless have been evil twins for a long time. It is unlikely they will ever break up. That is okay. Just know that your friends of Love and Let Go, who are on your team, will work with you to guide your thinking and actions.

Reinforce your belief that it is time to take action…just one step at a time.

## STOP, START, OR CONTINUE

> "People mistakenly assume that their thinking is done by their head; it is actually done by the heart, which first dictates the conclusion, then commands the head to provide the reasoning that will defend it."
>
> — Anthony de Mello, *Jesuit priest and psychotherapist*

At least once a year when I led the corporate team, we would do the exercise of Stop, Start or Continue. We spent time writing down what we should stop doing, what we should start doing, and what we should continue doing. We did this as individuals and also as a team. We shared the results with each other to better understand each other's point of view.

Why bother doing this?

Two main reasons this is important:

First, since we are all creatures of habit, we add tasks and routines to our daily life, without considering the overall impact on our life.

*…we add tasks and routines to our daily life, without considering the overall impact on our life.*

In reality, what happens is we keep adding to our things-to-do list: new tasks, more reports to read, more key stats to gather, and more projects. Rarely do we eliminate any ongoing task or project. We just keep doing, doing, doing. The list of what we "feel" needs to be accomplished quickly becomes unmanageable.

If you are overwhelmed with little time to do what you want to do, consider all the tasks and routines you do now. Have you ever thought about them, as a whole?

Second, we rarely stop to think about what is working well and what is not working well. Why do we not take the time to think about these two questions? You already know the answer: We are so caught up in the day-to-day activities of life that we just do not dedicate enough thinking time to assess what works and what doesn't.

So how does this exercise help with procrastination?

I can guarantee you that you are doing things that no longer serve you, take up valuable time, and run in autopilot mode. Of the three categories (Stop, Start, Continue), spend some extra time thinking about what you need to STOP doing. Think about something you need to stop doing or can delegate.

Once you commit to yourself that you will stop doing task X, then your next question is…what should I start?

## EXAMPLES OF THIS CONCEPT:

The first example is on a personal level…the dreaded "going to the gym."

A commonly held belief is that people do not exercise because they do not have enough time or cannot fit a trip to the gym into their schedule. In this example, could one stop watching TV or surfing the Internet (Stop) for one hour at night, go to bed one hour earlier (Start), and then get up an hour earlier to make it to the gym (Start)?

Think creatively for solutions to your own Stop/Start question.

Test some to see if they will work.

The second example is on a business level…your email in-box is overflowing, making it hard to find emails you need to respond to, overwhelming you, and you can't get caught up. This results in missed deadlines or priorities. So in this example, could one learn how to effectively manage the in-box (Start) so the feeling of "out of control" goes away (Stop)? A clean in-box is an amazing feeling. If you have never had that, check out Leo Babauta's article at www.zenhabits.net/email-sanity. You will be glad you did.

## EXERCISE #8 – *Your List of Stop, Start and Continue*

### Stop

1. _____

2. _____

3. _____

4. _____

### Start

1. _____

2. _____

3. _____

4. _____

### Continue

1. _____

2. _____

3._____

4. _____

Template is available at www.YourProcrastinationCoach.com/
free-for-you

Chapter

5

"*The moment you commit and quit holding back, all sorts of unforeseen incidents, meetings, and material assistance will rise up to help you. The simple act of commitment is a powerful magnet for help.*"

— Napoleon Hill, *American author*

## REFLECT AND DETERMINE YOUR PRIORITIES

**You will want** to review and update your Procrastination Log periodically. By doing this, you will shape your thinking and impact your procrastination habits for the long term.

Create a binder in which to keep this information. Place the binder where you will actively see it on your desk.

Analyzing the procrastinated items provides insights about your patterns.

Mark the date when you <u>add</u> an item and the date you <u>complete</u> it so you can see your progress over time. Or as you complete items, take them off the list, and add new ones as needed. Use the tool in the way that works best for you.

Allow thirty to sixty minutes to answer the following questions.

Take time to reflect on your answers; you will find that by analyzing YOUR information you will glean some insights about your priorities, your feelings, your consequences, and your possible action plans.

> *Key Learning: The purpose of the Procrastination Log is to become more aware of exactly how procrastination is impacting your life in a total sense ... a holistic view. After completing it, look for patterns of behavior or habits.*

## EXERCISE #9 – *Analysis of Your Procrastination Log*

1. What thoughts come to mind when you review the list...seeing it in its totality? Is it overwhelming? If yes, why?

_____

_____

_____

_____

2. Does one item POP out at you as PRIORITY? Which one is it?

_____

_____

3. What patterns do you see? For example, do you have a hard time starting a project or finishing one, or do most items revolve around a specific area in your life such as job or health, or is there a category such as decisions or projects that seems to be prevalent?

_____

_____

_____

4. Jot down thoughts about how you feel about your distracting tasks that are filling your time.

_____

_____

5. Can you think of a routine or system that would help you eliminate procrastination for specific tasks?

_____

_____

_____

_____

6. Will you keep this list in a safe place and refer to it frequently, so that you can update it?

_____

_____

## YOUR HABITS ARE ALWAYS ON THE LINE

*"Successful people aren't born that way. They become successful by establishing the habit of doing things unsuccessful people do not like to do. The successful people don't always like these things themselves; they just get on and do them."*

— Author unknown

Recently, I was sitting in a Starbucks and overhead the conversation of three women who were loud and animated. They were discussing a business vendor they all knew. You know how close those tables can be, and you don't want to hear others' conversations but it happens. Here was the reason they were so animated:

One woman said, "He's late again."

The other one said, "He's late on everything—his paperwork, his part of the project, his appointments, his client proposals—just everything. I hate doing business with him."

The third woman stated it very clearly when she said, "I know, but he is good at his specialty—but the way he runs his business aggravates me, too. He will never change. We just have to deal with it."

Obviously, this guy and his business had quite a reputation for not being dependable and for not ever delivering anything on time.

Those who did business with him valued his expertise in his industry, but were annoyed by his bad habits.

Your habits create a pattern.

Where are you on the scale below—of being on top of things or not?

If you have staff, where are they? They reflect an image of your business to the public, as well.

What is your consistent pattern with others?

**What is your consistent pattern with others on 1-7 scale?**

| Improvement Needed: (1) | Has It Together: (7) |
|---|---|
| Low level of trust | High level of trust |
| Always late (appointments, proposals, etc.) | Always on time |
| Cannot count on their commitment | Commitments always honored |
| Inconsistent with most actions | Consistent actions |
| Not dependable, great with excuses | Very dependable |

Thinking about your own habits—good and bad—is not easy.

But take a moment to think of someone you know in business who exemplifies having it all together, who is consistently on the right side of the preceding scale for themselves, their business, their employees, and their reputation.

## EXERCISE #10 – *Success Characteristics of Others*

Some questions to think about:

• What do they do differently?

_____

_____

• What drives to them to be consistently on that right side of the scale?

_____

_____

• How did they learn to think differently?

_____

_____

• What benefits do they enjoy in their business as a result of their world-class reputation? Benefits like these: more customers, more referrals, more profits

_____

_____

You have the picture in your head. Now let's think about you:

• Exactly what steps would you and your business need to take and do differently to model this behavior?

_____

_____

• Where are you now when you look at the chart? Put an X and a date where you are on the line.

_____

_____

Sometimes it is hard to be honest with ourselves on the concept of commitment, dependability, and honoring our word. Would we stand out in a crowd (or our industry) if we had standards that we lived up to consistently every day? We all know the answer is YES!

We know the flip side of the proverbial coin is procrastination.

If others were to ask YOUR business associates, clients, family, and friends, what would they say about you and your business?

## WHY DOES IT MATTER?

You might be asking yourself that very question: Why does it even matter?

None of us are perfect. But here's the real question: Is there a pattern in your life as to how people see you or think of you?

As a procrastination coach, I assess and evaluate my client's habits and then correlate how they act with *their* definition of success. Usually their habits and where they want to be in life are in alignment. For example, one of my clients is not ambitious, not focused on end results, and takes a lot of time to finish tasks. He wonders why he is not more successful in his career.

A person who is consistently late with time, deliverables, and meeting commitments is simply not honoring themselves or the other person. They are procrastinating: avoiding or putting off something that needs to be done.

On the scale, my suggestion to you is to consider two things: Know where you are on the scale line and determine what you need to do to move your X on that line.

The reality of life is that many of us are in the middle section most of the time and occasionally stray to the left or stray to the right, depending on the tasks before us.

## WHAT CAN I DO ABOUT MY PATTERN OF PROCRASTINATION?

There are three steps to consider:

1. Self-awareness. Be honest with yourself about habits or actions you display that truly aggravate your family, friends, customers, and vendors.

2. Vision. Capture the picture in your head of how it could be improved, could look different, and more important — could feel different. It is okay to look around you to see who is doing it well and model them. That method is one of the best ways to learn.

3. Action. Make a commitment to take on one or two of these persistent bad habits and replace them with new ones that better serve you, your business, and your customer.

Your habits are always "on the line." The question is where on that line you want to be. You have the power to decide.

## DIFFICULTIES AND DELAYS

*"Delay is the deadliest form of denial."*

— C. Northcote Parkinson, *British historian*

Sometimes we procrastinate because of circumstances beyond our control. We let those circumstances affect our emotions and motivation. And we stop.

Has it happened to you that some event or some ill-spoken words impacted your energy level or motivation? And you just stopped.

You know exactly what I am referring to. You start a project and then encounter an unforeseen situation which causes difficulties or delays. The project becomes more complex than you had anticipated. More decisions need to be made and you feel like you need more information, which then causes more delays. All this adds up to you being frustrated.

You are now procrastinating on making decisions, talking to those involved, or taking any action. You feel better by just avoiding doing anything! (Or so you think!)

It has happened to all of us at one point or another.

## OVERCOMING THE EXTERNAL FACTORS

So what do you do? Consider following the steps listed:

**First step:** Be aware you have stopped making progress. Think about it and acknowledge it.

**Second step:** Revisit the original goal of why you were doing the project in the first place. What were you trying to accomplish? By reminding yourself of the goal, you can begin to think about how to move forward rather than remaining stuck.

**Third step:** Think about a small step that will get you out of the rut and restart the momentum. Any small step will do!

Make a promise to yourself that you will do this small step. Do it today or determine when in your calendar you could take this **"one small step."**

Don't worry about whether it is the best next step at this point.

It is important to locate a day and time in your calendar when you will commit to doing this small step. Enter the task, so it is in writing. Make the commitment to yourself that you will honor this commitment and do it.

When you are stuck on taking action and it has taken up permanent residence inside your head, then you have to consciously do something to un-stick it.

If you don't take action, the task will remain in your thoughts, producing guilt or resentment. You don't want that to happen, do you?

Think about something you have procrastinated on due to an external factor...and take action now using the three steps outlined above.

Are you ready? If not now, then when?

Chapter

**6**

*Before you begin a thing, remind yourself that difficulties and delays quite impossible to foresee are ahead...You can only see one thing clearly, and that is your goal. Form a mental vision of that and cling to it through thick and thin."*
— *Kathleen Norris, American author*

## TYING THE SUCCESS FACTORS TOGETHER

**Once you have** prioritized your list, you know the one item you need to work on first. But oftentimes, just the identification of which one is not enough to get us started and motivated.

The real secret to reshaping your thinking on procrastination is understanding *why* you didn't procrastinate in specific tasks in your life. You had specific beliefs about those tasks. You had specific steps to accomplish those tasks. You had habits or routines in place that were automatic and not questioned. Essentially, you simply took action.

What we want to accomplish is adjusting your belief system and your routines to make a difference on your procrastinated items.

What is the best way to do this?

1. Think through your beliefs
2. Understand what you would do to alter those beliefs
3. Systematize them through standard action steps
4. Repeat the routine to create automatic habits
5. Incorporate the process into your new belief system

Charles Duhigg, author of *The Power of Habit*, explains in his book how habits are formed. He writes that our brain converts a series of actions into an automatic routine. The brain actually wants to make almost any routine into a habit, as it allows the brain some downtime, thus conserving mental energy.

> *"The brain goes through a three-step loop. First there is a cue, a trigger that tells your brain to go into automatic mode and which habit to use. Then there is the routine, which can be physical, mental, or emotional. Finally, there is the reward, which helps your brain figure out if this particular loop is worth remembering for the future. Over time, this loop — cue, routine, reward; cue, routine, reward—becomes more and more automatic. A habit is born."*

— Charles Duhigg, *The Power of Habit*

Habits are important because the brain is not participating in decision making, thus avoiding introducing fears or anxieties. We can't change the cues, but we CAN change the routines, which will impact the outcome.

You have to create the system or routine, a series of steps that will take away all the excuses and set the action plans in motion.

## CREATING THE ROUTINE TO FOLLOW

Go back to your Procrastination Log and review your number-one-priority task you want to accomplish.

Think about how to break it down into manageable steps. Keep it simple. Think whether you need anyone to help you—

someone to whom you could delegate tasks. If there's no such person, then look at your calendar now and block out time to begin work on your number-one-priority item.

To further illustrate this important step of pulling it all together, I will share an example from one of my clients, Julie:

Julie hated going to local networking events. She did not like going in the front door, knowing she would be meeting a bunch of strangers and making small talk. Julie had been in business for one year. She was self-conscious and just did not like networking. Julie knew she needed to do so to gain new clients and build her business. We worked together to create a system that became a HABIT that resulted in success!

Originally it had three steps but then progressed to five. She no longer procrastinates in this area, as she follows the system. Her brain has accepted this routine, so Julie easily follows along.

1. At the first of each month, she has logged in her calendar to find networking events in her area, and logs them into her calendar.

2. She has all her networking paraphernalia in one place, all the materials she would take to a networking event. Advance preparation makes it easy to gather her materials and head out to the networking event: business cards, brochures, notebook, pen, names of people met at past events.

3. She set up a special section in her closet for her "networking outfits."

4. She created a list of three icebreaker questions to ask new people she meets.

5. She created a follow-up system for when she got back to her office: loading the names and any special information to remember into Outlook Contacts and then sending an email saying "good to meet you."

In a sense, it is a checklist she knows she will consistently follow. She is still not totally comfortable with networking, but over time, she has increased her confidence. She continues to attend networking events, as she knows that doing so will build her business. She has a system to follow. Through repetition, she has become more effective at networking.

By creating this system, she "took the thinking out of it," and as the author Charles Duhigg says, the brain can no longer introduce fears and anxieties.

## EXERCISE #11 – *Tackling the #1 Priority Item*

Create your checklist on your **#1 priority** procrastinated item from the Procrastination Log to begin creating the good habits needed to stop procrastinating.

Again, you may want to keep the Procrastination Log and these pages in a three-ring binder.

Create your steps by brainstorming first, then narrow down to the important three to five steps that will provide you momentum and help you become unstuck.

I recommend you create one page per procrastinated item. Download the template at www.YourProcrastinationCoach.com/free-for-you.

Try out the newly created routine to see if there are any tweaks that need to occur. The repetition of the routine will make it an automatic habit. Only doing something once will not make it a

**NEW ROUTINE**

| Date Created: |
|---|
| Date Started: |
| Date Review: |

Description of what I am procrastinating on:

| |
|---|

Consequences if do not take action:

| |
|---|

Benefits if I do it consistently:

| |
|---|

How will I feel:

| |
|---|

How will I celebrate when I am doing this consistently?

| |
|---|

Steps I need to take consistently, thus creating the routine:

| 1. |
|---|
| 2. |
| 3. |
| 4. |
| 5. |

habit. Awareness and repetition is the key.

**Key learning: Knowing the routine will help me to stay on track and overcome procrastination in that area of my life.**

Key Questions:

1. How did it feel when you wrote down your steps?

_____

_____

2. Will you keep this information in a binder and refer to it periodically? If so, how often? (Put the timing in your calendar NOW.) Where will you keep it?

_____

_____

## PROCRASTINATION AND PROMISES

*"Self-trust is the first secret to success."*
— Ralph Waldo Emerson, *American Poet*

Procrastination feels so bad. We do not trust ourselves.

Procrastinators want to make progress but cannot. They get distracted with other, less important, tasks until the deadline is upon them. Then they somehow get quickly focused on what needs to be done at the last minute.

Sometimes it is successful, the deadline is met, and everyone is happy. Sometimes it is not successful.

The pressure and angst create high anxiety, causing an emotional roller coaster for the procrastinator and others around them.

Sound familiar?

We all know the promises you make to yourself.

"This time will be different. I will start on the project right away. I will get out a calendar and work backwards with the timeline and action steps. I know I can do it this time."

"I am busy doing all these other activities, and I should be working on Project X. When I finish with these other activities, then I will work on Project X."

"I think I have enough time to pull this off so that no one finds out I have procrastinated."

The procrastinator is desperate, feels guilty, and holds on to the hope of being able to get by doing just enough. They do not want anyone to know of their dilemma and will sometimes present the image of progress, when they are behind in the project. Sometimes they avoid people, meetings, and phone calls as a result.

*What it boils down to is—will you do what you said you were going to do?*

Your first promise to keep is to yourself. Keep track of your promises. Those made to others and to yourself. Write them down to hold yourself accountable: You will think twice about whether you are able to honor that promise or not.

Breaking the cycle—can it be done? Yes, with conscious effort.

Acknowledge that procrastination is not due to laziness, lack of discipline, or disorganization. Instead, be conscious of the next time you procrastinate.

## EXERCISE #12 – *Understanding Promises and Trust*

Ask yourself:

1. Why am I delaying or avoiding this task or project?

_____

_____

2. How can I do this differently? What steps do I need to take and when?

_____

_____

3. What do I need to do to be successful and to keep this promise of completion on time?

_____

_____

4. Whom do I know that I trust and will hold me accountable?

_____

_____

5. If I have success, can I repeat it with future tasks and projects?

_____

_____

Suggested process to follow, using an accountability partner:

1. Choose a small action to get in motion on something you have not completed but need to.
2. Tell someone you trust that you are working on this. Declare the next task you will need to do.
3. Let that person know when you have accomplished the task—consider them an Accountability Coach, even if they have not signed on for that role!
4. Repeat the process…taking it a step at a time.

Eventually you will get there! Most important, honor your promises. Very few people do on a consistent basis.

Be dependable.

## How Procrastination Keeps You from Getting New Clients

*"One reason so few of us achieve what we truly want is that we never direct our focus, we never concentrate our power. Most people dabble their way through life never deciding to master anything in particular."*

— Anthony Robbins, *American motivational leader*

On many occasions in working with small business clients, I am told how hard it is for them to get new clients. Being a business owner myself, I totally understand.

When I inquire about their process of attracting new clients and following up with people who could be potential clients, I get blank stares and a few "ums" and "ers."

The lifeblood of a business is the client.

As a business coach, I care about my clients' customers. I want to know how many new clients they obtain in a month and how many they retain. Based on the type of business, the average number of new customers added in a month, and the total size of the client base, I can make a guesstimate on the health of that business. My next usual question of the business owner is if they use a set system or routine to follow up with potential clients—again I usually get a blank stare.

Yes, they do follow up, but in a haphazard way.

Would that be considered procrastination or just lack of a system? Actually, it is both.

So let's talk about you and your process.

When you attend a networking event, you usually collect

business cards and meet some people who might be valuable to your business. What do you do with all that information?

## CREATE A SYSTEM THAT WORKS EVERY TIME

What would happen if:

1. You sent an email or handwritten note to that person within 24 hours of meeting them at the event?
2. You called that person within three days of the event to schedule a one-on-one meeting to explore if there is synergy between the two businesses?
3. You followed up that meeting with an email or handwritten note, recapping your meeting and asking for the business, within 24 hours?
4. You sent another email or note within seven days of that meeting highlighting the benefits of working with you? Frequency creates impact. They will remember you.

So, let's stop for a moment and count the contacts made within a two-week period of time. The total at this point is six interactions:

Initial meeting, #1 above, #2 above, face-to-face meeting, #3, and then #4 contact.

After six contacts, you should have a good idea if that person is interested and will be working with you.

Most people stop at the initial interaction and procrastinate on doing the other five interactions. You won't be one of those who fall into that trap, right?

Why do some stop at just one contact? Many say they are just too busy. That is possible…or they do not have a consistent system for follow-up…or have not seen the benefits of doing so.

At a networking event, your goal should be to have two to five meaningful conversations, not to collect business cards from everyone in the room. Doing that is unrealistic and not effective.

If you are a business owner, a salesperson, or someone looking for a job, I encourage you to create five or more steps based on what you know will work for you.

What is the system you need to create?

Write them out. Follow them for at least one month. After one month, determine if this is a habit you want to continue.

I bet you will say YES!

Chapter

7

*"Time is the coin of your life. It is the only coin you have, and only you can determine how it will be spent. Be careful lest you let other people spend it for you."*

— Carl Sandburg, *American poet*

## IT **IS** ALL ABOUT TIME

**As I stated** earlier in this book, how we view our time and use our time impacts our procrastination world.

I created a daily tool to keep me focused on what I want to accomplish. The tool, called the Capacity Sheet, helps me to avoid procrastinating. I usually complete the Capacity Sheet during the evening, as I plan the next day's priorities, appointments, reminders, and much more.

The four main benefits in using this sheet:
- Understanding the amount of hours I have available
- Forecasting accurately how long tasks will take
- Listing **just** the tasks (no more than 12) I can accomplish
- Reviewing at the end of the day how long tasks actually took to complete

Generally, we are not proficient in estimating how long tasks take to complete. Routinely, we will either underestimate or overestimate. This lack of proficiency hurts us when we try to accurately plan our day.

In the past, I would create a to-do list with fifty plus tasks to accomplish that day. It was not realistic. I was setting myself up to fail each day. No wonder I was burned out.

Now, when I plan, I am much more realistic as to what can be accomplished, given the capacity of time I have for that day. For example, if I have a network meeting in the morning and a client lunch appointment, then I can only count on four hours in the afternoon to accomplish other tasks. When thinking about what tasks need to be done, I ask myself, which are the two or three tasks I absolutely must complete that day?

What I ask myself is this: If I accomplish those two or three very important tasks, then I will deem the day a successful one. So which two or three are they?

## THE CAPACITY SHEET

| Date: | Capacity List (To do List that gets results) | | Approx Time Range to Do It | Actual Time To Do It |
|---|---|---|---|---|
| | Description | ✓Done | | |
| 1 | | | | |
| 2 | | | | |
| 3 | | | | |

I encourage you to download the Capacity Sheet from my website www.YourProcrastinationCoach.com/free-for-you. Print as many copies as you need.

## EXERCISE #13 – *Using the Capacity Sheet Effectively*

Use the Capacity Sheet (my version of the to-do list) for at least 10 days to gauge the impact of how you view time and priorities throughout the day. Use these questions as you use the Capacity Sheet and plan your upcoming days.

1. What are the 2-3 things I really need to get done tomorrow—the big, important, impactful (tasks/decisions, discussions, etc) that will make a difference in my life or business?

The goal is to shape your thoughts as follows:

**If I get those 2 or 3 things done tomorrow, then I will feel that it was a successful/accomplished day.**

2. Write down the item in column 1 (Description) and put a STAR or 1, 2, 3, in the last column if it is a priority item.

3. Fill in the rest of your day on what other items you want to accomplish. Try to limit yourself to 12 items. If you have more, you may want to create a separate sheet called "Brain Dump/Master List" to pick off those items you want to work on each day. Or realize that you will not be able to add it to tomorrow's sheet, but determine which day in the near future you could accomplish this task. Create a Capacity Sheet for that day in the future with that task already filled in.

4. Capture the appointments you have committed for the day in lower right corner. Doing so will help you to know that the time is not available to work on tasks. Just write down time and appointment name. Be brief.

5. Add in notes to yourself on what NOT to commit to on that day in the bottom lower left corner. All you need to write is a few key words. For example, if you are going to a meeting that you *know* you will be asked to do a task

that you absolutely do not want to commit to, then write it down thus promising to *yourself* that you will say NO.

6. I am often asked if this sheet can be completed electronically. It can, but….. I recommend that you use the paper version for at least 10 days and be engaged with the totality of the information at-a-glance.

7. **This is the most important step of the Capacity Sheet.** Guess or estimate (!) how long it will take you to complete the tasks you entered. Be mindful as you go through the day to see how long it really does take to do that task. The greater awareness you have on how long it takes to do these types of tasks, the better you will manage your time and what you are able to accomplish. For example, if I write a weekly blog, then how long does it realistic take to complete? For me, it is two hours to create the idea, begin writing, do research, write some more, and then correct the drafts. If I add it to my calendar and only block one hour, then again, I am setting myself up to fail.

The more frequently you do a task, the more proficient you become on the amount of time needed.

Your goal is to be able to reliably predict how long tasks and appointments will take. Once you can do that with a high degree of accuracy, then you will have more control over your calendar.

There may be days when you have no "open capacity" of time. When someone asks you to complete a task that day, you are able to reliably respond "I am sorry that I do not have capacity".

Another example: a salesperson I coach will block out one hour each day to do follow-up calls. He is persistent to make outgoing calls until the hour is up. He doesn't worry about how many calls were made, only that he honored the full one hour of phone call activity.

Capture any AHA's that you gleaned from this exercise.

_____

_____

_____

The better you can forecast your time and tasks, the better you can manage your day and truly understand your capacity.

Your transformation will be when you can successfully plan your day and week, getting done what you need to get done, given the time available to do so.

There is an audio CD as part of the three CD set that explains in more details and with more examples on using the Capacity Sheet.

## CONCLUSION – NEXT STEPS TO TAKE

## CONGRATULATIONS!

**You made it** to the finish line, and I hope you have learned that SUCCESSFULLY FAILING at procrastination is all about awareness, thinking, planning, and creating and following the steps to make it a habit.

Essentially, you are replacing the procrastination habit of avoidance or delay with an automatic habit. The key to success is substituting a new action and routine in some very important areas of your life.

When you examine your life closely, you will find automatic habits in other areas of your life. Learning how to apply this habit-changing concept and technique to the more challenging areas of your life will provide a process you can repeat over and over.

Failing consistently (and successfully) at procrastination is your ultimate goal: to be able to say, "I used to procrastinate a lot in my life, but now it is just occasional!"

Using this book, you have accomplished the following:

• You identified areas where you don't procrastinate.

• You acknowledged emotions that are not serving you in

your life.

- You figured out whether you have a pattern of "not starting" or "not finishing."
- You prioritized what areas of your life are bothering you most.
- You began the process of creating a system for your number-one priority area.
- You learned the consequences for continuing on your old path with no changes.
- You saw the benefits of changing habits and routines, one area at a time.
- You learned that you can shift your thinking for any challenge ahead — just by working through it.
- You gained the feeling of a real sense of accomplishment — and the feeling that you can do this.

Most important, you have learned a new skill and enhanced your personal development.

In a short period of time, you have delved into a habit that has impacted your life for a long time. I honor you for your commitment to think, plan, and act!

# Resources

## WHAT'S NEXT IF YOU WANT TO KNOW MORE?

**If you found** value in this book, you may want to explore other ways to build on what you have learned.

## TELE-CLASSES

Check out www.YourProcrastinationCoach.com or www. LaurenMidgley.com for upcoming small-group classes.

I conduct monthly tele-classes so that you do not lose momentum in your learning. The class size is purposefully kept small so that everyone gets personal attention. Please join us! The class addresses this material, as well as other information that gets at the heart of procrastination.

The classes are conducted by phone as a group, generally over a three-to-five-week time frame.

## ONE-ON-ONE HELP

Sometimes it is helpful to work with someone one on one to help you specifically on your challenges and on understanding how this habit is impacting your life. If you are looking for an Accountability Coach to help keep you on track, email me at Lauren@LaurenMidgley.com to share what you are looking to accomplish and in what time frame.

## Blog

I research the topic and routinely share my findings. Check back frequently for updates at www.YourProcrastinationCoach.com.

## Weekly email

Sign up for my weekly email at www.YourProcrastination-Coach.com. These insightful emails offer a One Minute Tip, a Motivational Quote, and a Challenge Question. Those who have received it absolutely love the information and find that the emails impact their thinking and focus.

## Free Documents

At www.YourProcrastinationCoach.com, you will find many templates that will help you, such as the Capacity Sheet, the Procrastination Log and much more.

## Audio, Workbook, and Journal

I developed a more in-depth home-study course for those who cannot make the tele-classes and prefer to work at their own pace. Check the website for details.

## Excellent Books

I am an avid reader on the topic of procrastination; other authors are passionate about this topic as well.

*The Procrastinator's Handbook: Mastering the Art of Doing It Now*, by Rita Emmett
*Work Less, Make More*, by Jennifer White
*5 a.m. & Already Behind*, by Dr. Don Kennedy
*Procrastination*, by Jane Burka and Lenora Yuen
*The Now Habit*, by Neil Fiore, PhD
*Overachievement*, by John Eliot, PhD

*The Power of Habit*, by Charles Duhigg
*Failing Forward*, by John Maxwell

Good luck on your journey to impact the habit of procrastination. With tools, the right mind-set, and a plan, you CAN **SUCCESSFULLY FAIL AT PROCRASTINATION**.

Feel free to email me at Lauren@LaurenMidgley.com or call me at 817-965-4244 to share with me your progress. I can guarantee you that I will be your biggest cheerleader.

# About
# the Author

**Lauren Midgley**, business strategy coach for franchise owners
and entrepreneurs, is effective at helping people tackle the procrastination habit. Her style and approach impact their thinking
to get RESULTS!

Lauren worked with franchisees and entrepreneurs to shift
their thinking, create effective strategies, and improve their businesses. She saw many business owners, managers, and employees
struggle every day due to procrastination. They put off their key
goals, tasks, discussions, and projects due to distractions and a
lack of focus on the priorities. Procrastination was RAMPANT!
Productivity was LOW!

It is no secret that when procrastination occurs, it stems from
a lack of clarity about what needs to be accomplished or from
knowing an unpleasant task is ahead.

Lauren started Courage to Succeed Coaching in 2010, after
having spent more than twenty years working with small business owners to build their businesses. She saw firsthand how the
habit of procrastination crippled businesses, as well as herself.
As a result, she became a procrastination coach. As a speaker,
business coach, and author, Lauren is passionate on the topic of
procrastination. In her speaking engagements and workshops,
she inspires the audience to think differently and to focus on
the possibilities for improvement. She is an enthusiastic speaker

who easily relates to the audience because she is a "recovering procrastinator."

Lauren provides solid content customized to the audience so they can enjoy the information and learn techniques they can use right away.

She earned her MBA from Golden Gate University and her undergraduate marketing degree from Arizona State University. Lauren achieved the Certified Franchise Executive designation from the International Franchise Association. Lauren is active with Toastmasters and National Speaker Association. She lives in Colleyville, Texas, with her two teenage children.

Websites: www.YourProcrastinationCoach.com and www.LaurenMidgley.com

Lauren welcomes your feedback and questions on this book and topic.

You can reach her at:

Email: Lauren@LaurenMidgley.com
Phone: 817-965-4244

42760791R00059

Made in the USA
Lexington, KY
04 July 2015